Never Never Lands

Western Australian Outback

To chronicle the creation stories of the city, Unknown Fields head off on a dust-blown road trip across Australia, into the vast and mysterious interior of this remote island continent in search of its ancient tribal hinterlands and its immense techno-landscapes. Beneath the Southern Cross, machines harvest the earth for the precious ingredients of our daily lives. We stalk mechanical beasts the size of buildings and explore excavations the size of cities. Here, in the Never Never, are the resource territories of the city, a land of rich geology, endless horizons and mining pits so large that they generate their own weather systems. Towering mountains of tailings, remade landforms, terraced valleys and artificial lakes all take shape from this distributed ground. Violent gestures of accelerated geology create landscapes of erasure, excavation and re-articulation.

    For this book, Unknown Fields travel 1km beneath the surface of the earth in search of gold, to survey and laser-scan the technological incisions that release it from the ground. We follow tunnels winding below Australia's red crust and stand at the base of the mega pits that are cut through the narrative landscape of the Dreamtime, the creation mythology of the Aboriginal Australians. Stories and ceremonies of dreaming beings that once formed the sacred sites of mountain ranges and river-beds are now spun with the ghosts of modern technologies, family heirlooms and financial fictions. Territories once mapped into surfaces of Aboriginal dot paintings are now depicted on screen in the digital point clouds of geology survey scans. Stories from two indigenous authors act as our Dreamtime guide as we drift across the grounds of traditional creation, before diving deep to follow a new subterranean songline, one created from underground mine computer models and laser survey data. We retrace a constellation of gold artefacts scattered across the earth back through mine pits and tunnels to their origin in ore bodies deep below. Roughly 0.034grams of this landscape is locked away in each of our mobile phones, charged and quietly vibrating. We all carry a little piece of Australia in our pockets.

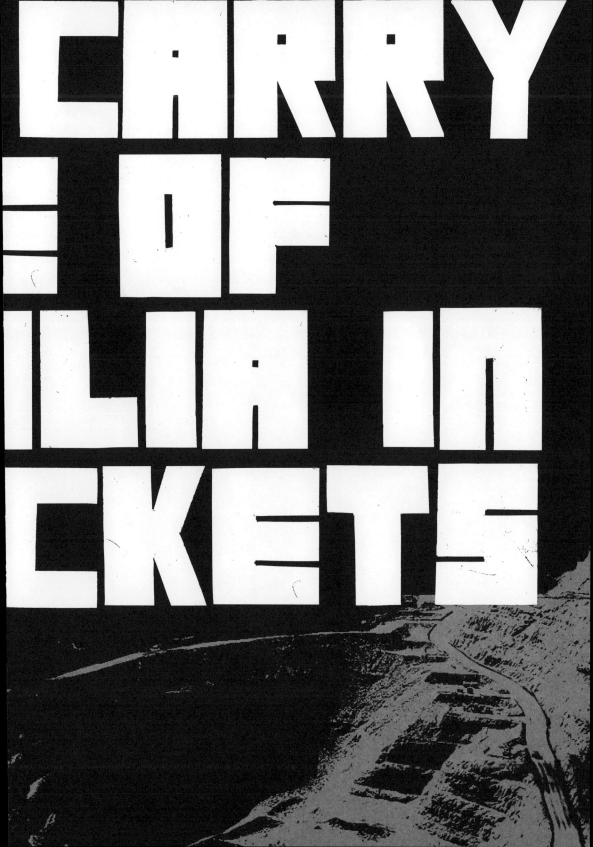

Distributed Ground

Our city of gold casts a long shadow across
the earth. Here lies the silent twin: the void
where a landform once was. An ancient landscape
scattered and redistributed, remade into bullion
in a vault, a grandmother's ring, a gangster's
tooth, electrical connections, a gold-plated
revolver, a haul of Roman coins in a museum or
gold flakes in a shot glass. From the ground
comes a catalogue of gold objects. Every object
leaves a trace and the fluctuations of the
gold price on the market sends ripples through
the earth. The territories of Australia become
atomised into a constellation of glistening
things scattered around the world. The dust
of Australia blows gold.

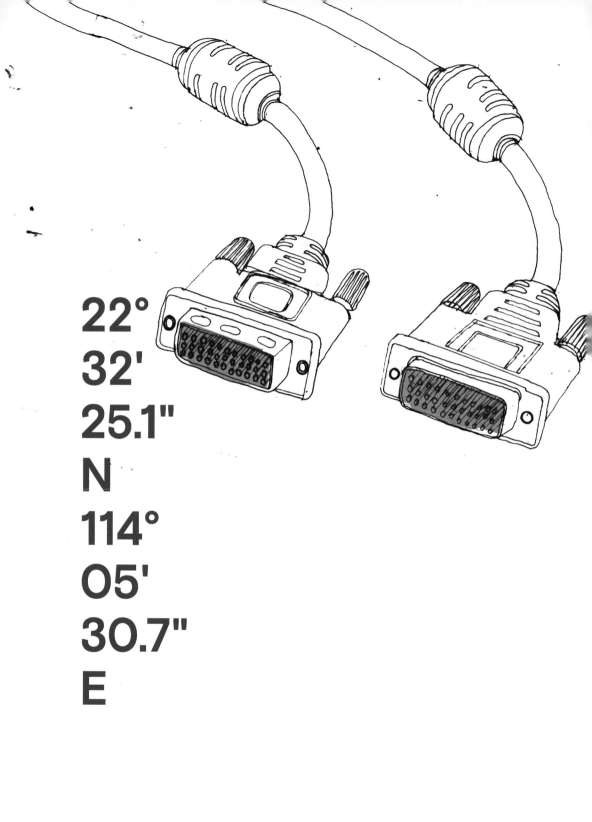

22°
32'
25.1"
N
114°
05'
30.7"
E

22°
43'
59.1"
N
114°
13'
01.9"
E

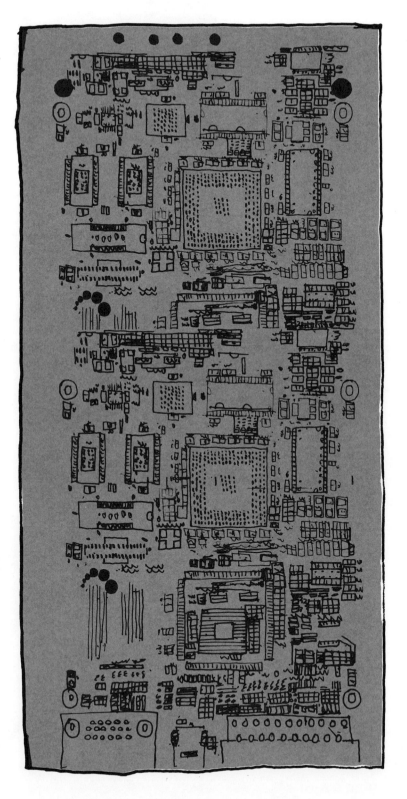

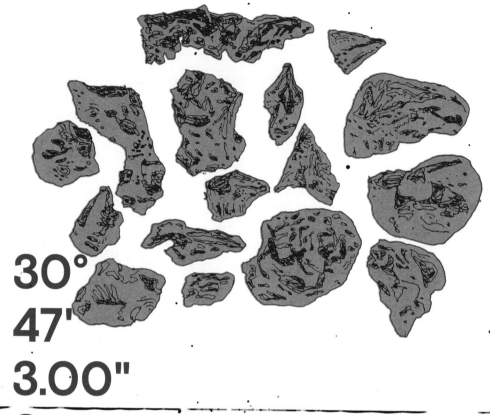

30°
47'
3.00"
S
121°
30'
30.25"
E

33°

53'

32.6"

N

118°

13'

54.4

W

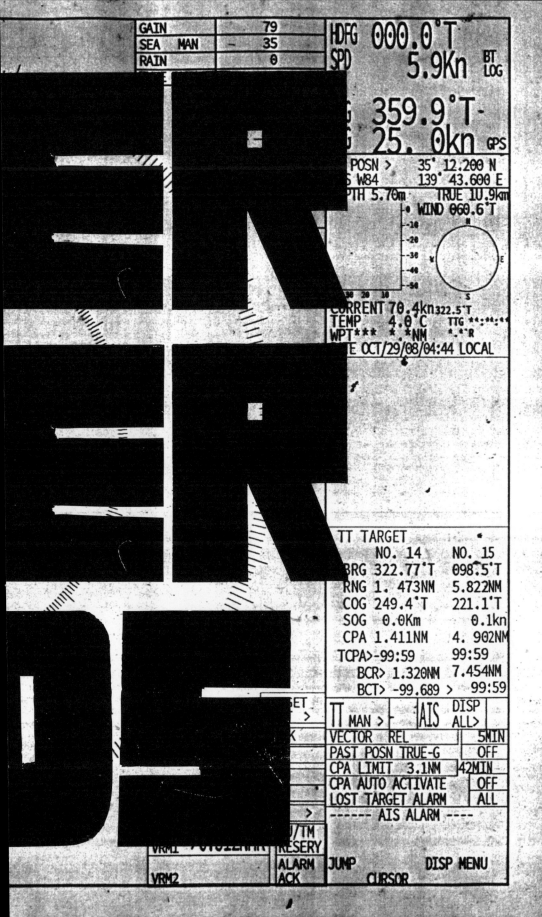

GAIN		79
SEA MAN	–	35
RAIN		0

HDFG 000.0°T
SPD   5.9Kn BT LOG

359.9°T-
25. 0kn GPS

POSN >   35° 12.200 N
W84   139° 43.600 E
TH 5.70m   TRUE 10.9km
• WIND 060.6°T
-10
-20
-30
-40
-50

CURRENT 70.4kn 322.5°T
TEMP   4.0°C   TTG **:**:**
WPT***   * *NM   *.*°R
E OCT/29/08/04:44 LOCAL

TT TARGET
          NO. 14   NO. 15
BRG 322.77°T   098.5°T
RNG 1. 473NM   5.822NM
COG 249.4°T   221.1°T
SOG 0.0Km   0.1kn
CPA 1.411NM   4. 902NM
TCPA>-99:59   99:59
   BCR> 1.320NM 7.454NM
   BCT> -99.689 >   99:59

TT MAN >   AIS   DISP ALL>

VECTOR REL		5MIN
PAST POSN TRUE-G		OFF
CPA LIMIT 3.1NM	42MIN
CPA AUTO ACTIVATE		OFF
LOST TARGET ALARM		ALL

------ AIS ALARM ----

VRM1
RESERV
ALARM   JUMP   DISP MENU
ACK
VRM2   CURSOR

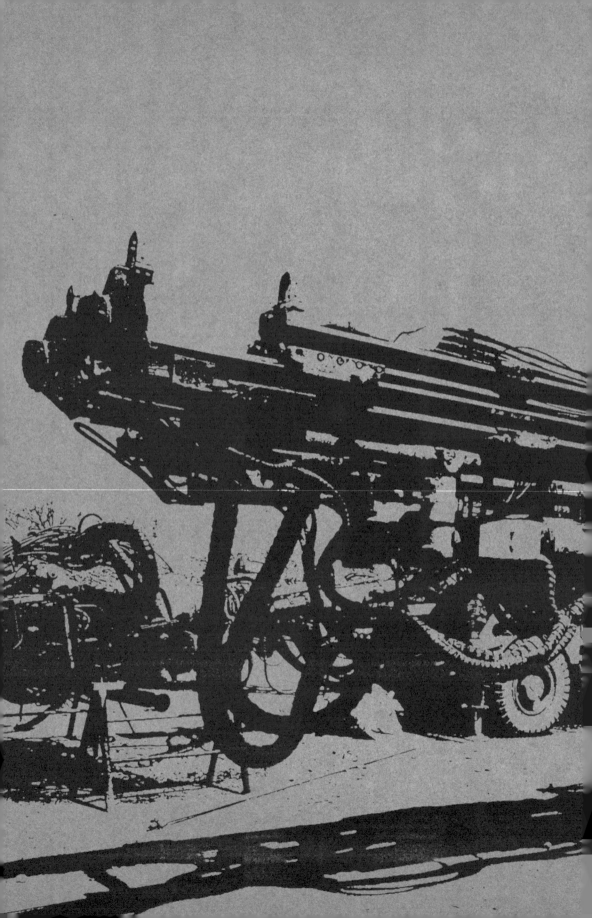

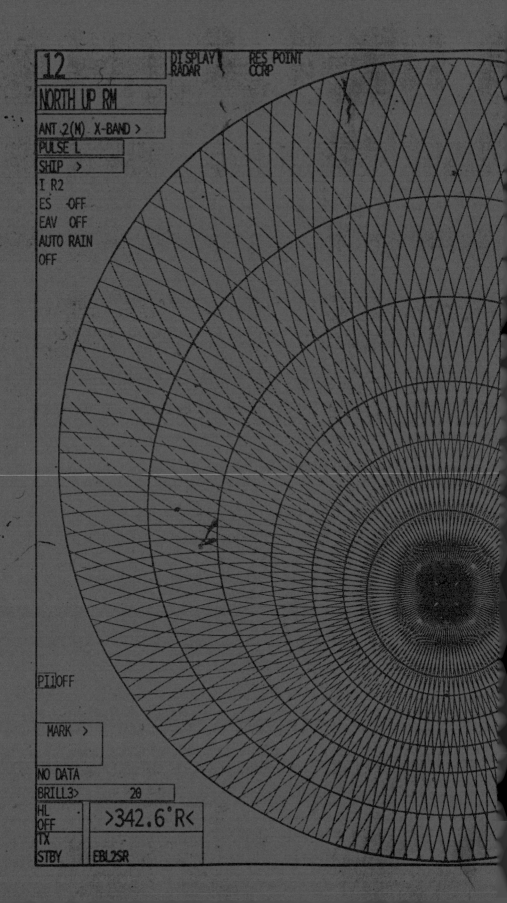

12

NORTH UP RM

ANT 2(M) X-BAND >
PULSE L
SHIP >
I R2
ES OFF
EAV OFF
AUTO RAIN
OFF

DISPLAY   RES POINT
RADAR   CCRP

PI1OFF

MARK >

NO DATA

BRILL3>   20

HL
OFF   >342.6°R<
TX
STBY   EBL2SR

When the Earth Was Soft

Words by Indigenous Australian author
Alexis Wright. An extract from *Carpentaria*,
Giramondo, 2006.

From time immemorial

NATION CHANTS, BUT WE KNOW YOUR STORY ALREADY.
THE BELLS PEAL EVERYWHERE. CHURCH BELLS CALLING
THE FAITHFUL TO THE TABERNACLE WHERE THE GATES
OF HEAVEN WILL OPEN, BUT NOT FOR THE WICKED.
CALLING INNOCENT LITTLE BLACK GIRLS FROM A DISTANT
ABORIGINAL COMMUNITY WHERE THE WHITE DOVE BEARING
AN OLIVE BRANCH NEVER LANDS. LITTLE GIRLS WHO COME
BACK HOME AFTER CHURCH ON SUNDAY, WHO LOOK AROUND
THEMSELVES AT THE HUMAN FALLOUT AND ANNOUNCE
MATTER-OF-FACTLY, ARMAGEDDON BEGINS HERE.

The ancestral serpent, a creature larger than
storm clouds, came down from the stars, laden
with its own creative enormity. It moved
graciously – if you had been watching with the
eyes of a bird hovering in the sky far above
the ground. Looking down at the serpent's wet
body, glistening from the ancient sunlight,
long before man was a creature who could
contemplate the next moment in time. It came
down those billions of years ago, to crawl on
its heavy belly, all around the wet clay soils
in the Gulf of Carpentaria.
        Picture the creative serpent, scoring
deep into – scouring down through – the slippery
underground of the mudflats, leaving in its wake
the thunder of tunnels collapsing to form deep
sunken valleys. The sea water following in the
serpent's wake, swarming in a frenzy of tidal
waves, soon changed colour from ocean blue to

the yellow of mud. The water filled the swirling
tracks to form the mighty bending rivers spread
across the vast plains of the gulf country. The
serpent travelled over the marine plains, over
the salt flats, through the salt dunes, past the
mangrove forests and crawled inland. Then it went
back to the sea. And it came out at another spot
along the coastline and crawled inland and back
again. When it finished creating the many rivers
in its wake, it created one last river, no larger
or smaller than the others, a river which offers
no apologies for its discontent with people who
do not know it. This is where the giant serpent
continues to live deep down under the ground in a
vast network of limestone aquifers. They say its
being is porous; it permeates everything. It is
all around in the atmosphere and is attached to
the lives of the river people like skin.

        This tidal river snake of flowing mud
takes in breaths of a size that is difficult
to comprehend. Imagine the serpent's breathing
rhythms as the tide flows inland, edging towards
the spring waters nestled deeply in the gorges
of an ancient limestone plateau covered with
rattling grasses dried yellow from the prevailing
winds. Then with the outward breath, the tide
turns and the serpent flows back to its own
circulating mass of shallow waters in the giant
water basin in a crook of the mainland whose
sides separate it from the open sea.

        To catch this breath in the river you
need the patience of one who can spend days
doing nothing. If you wait under the rivergum
where those up-to-no-good mission-bred kids
accidentally hanged Cry-baby Sally, the tip of
the dead branch points to where you will see
how the serpent's breath fights its way through

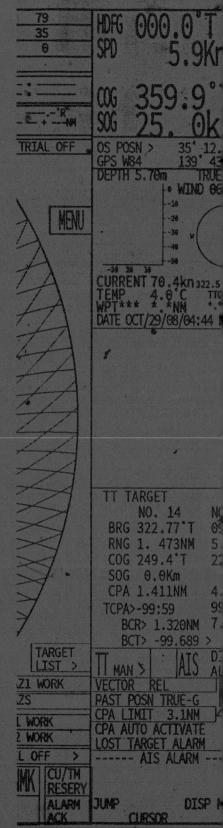

in a tunnel of wind, creating ripples that
shimmer silver, similar to the scales of a small,
nocturnal serpent, thrashing in anger whenever
the light hits its slippery translucent body,
making it writhe and wrench to escape back into
its natural environment of darkness.

   The inside knowledge about this river and
coastal region is the Aboriginal Law handed down
through the ages since time began. Otherwise,
how would one know where to look for the hidden
underwater courses in the vast flooding mud
plains, full of serpents and fish in the monsoon
season? Can someone who did not grow up in a
place that is sometimes under water, sometimes
bone-dry, know when the trade winds blowing off
the southern and northern hemispheres will merge
in summer? Know the moment of climatic change
better than they know themselves? Who fishes in
the yellow-coloured monsoonal runoff from the
drainages, with sheets of deep water pouring into
the wide rivers swollen over their banks, filling
vast plains with floodwaters? The cyclones linger
and regroup, the rain never stops pouring, but
the fat fish are abundant.

   It takes a particular kind of knowledge
to go with the river, whatever its mood. It is
about there being no difference between you and
the movement of water as it seasonally shifts its
tracks according to its own mood. A river that
spurns human endeavour in one dramatic gesture,
jilting a lover who has never really been known,
as it did to the frontier town built on its banks
in the hectic heyday of colonial vigour. A town
intended to serve as a port for the shipping
trade for the hinterland of Northern Australia.
AW

Subterranean Dreaming

Forged from the ancient supercontinent of Ur, the
ground of Western Australia is formed from some
of the oldest rocks on the planet. Aboriginal
dreamtime narratives speak of a time when the
ground was soft and creation beings shaped
mountains and rivers. When the rainbow serpent
slinked across the ground to create a river, and
a wild dog came to rest to form a mountain. Now
as the lights of the city wash out the sky the
songlines walked by these ancestral spirits are
sung anew with the tracks laid down by the beasts
of the mining industry. Here, as explosives,
diggers and drills replace the slow erosion of
rivers and winds, new stories are being told.
        The dreaming landscape that embodies the
creation stories of Aboriginal Australians is
overlaid with a vast infrastructure of resource
speculation and financial fictions. Geological
survey planes track back and forth, laser-
scanning the earth searching for the topographic
anomalies that indicate pockets of undiscovered
minerals in the ground. The millions of points
created by their scans are examined to determine
territories for core sampling. These in turn
give form to subterranean outcrops, features and
landmarks, bands and shards of material riches
under the dry red dirt.
        Aboriginal native title rights apply to
the surface of the earth but exclude the valuable
subsurface minerals which all belong to the
state. No one is yet singing the creation stories
of the ore body formations below ground. They are
voids in waiting, fragments of a country destined
to be taken away ship by ship.

Traditional dot paintings of dreamtime
stories have often been used to support land
rights claims but now the dots of the point
cloud data force a different type of claim on
the landscape. The technologies with which
this ground is surveyed, depicted and recorded
also become the means through which we claim
ownership over it. Constructed from 3D laser
scans, underground mine models and aerial survey
data, these point-cloud paintings, take us on a
subterranean journey — a worm's eye view of the
ore bodies, open-pits and tunnel excavations
of the gold mines of Western Australia. The
images recontextualise the data from economic
assessments of these landscapes within the
narrative of an alternative cultural reading.
Underneath our feet lies an inverted
landscape of glistening mineral-laden earth
and dormant nuggets destined to take the form
of the city's desires. This is a story about
a material valued above all others, but there
exists a parallel story, about the value of
this landscape untouched.

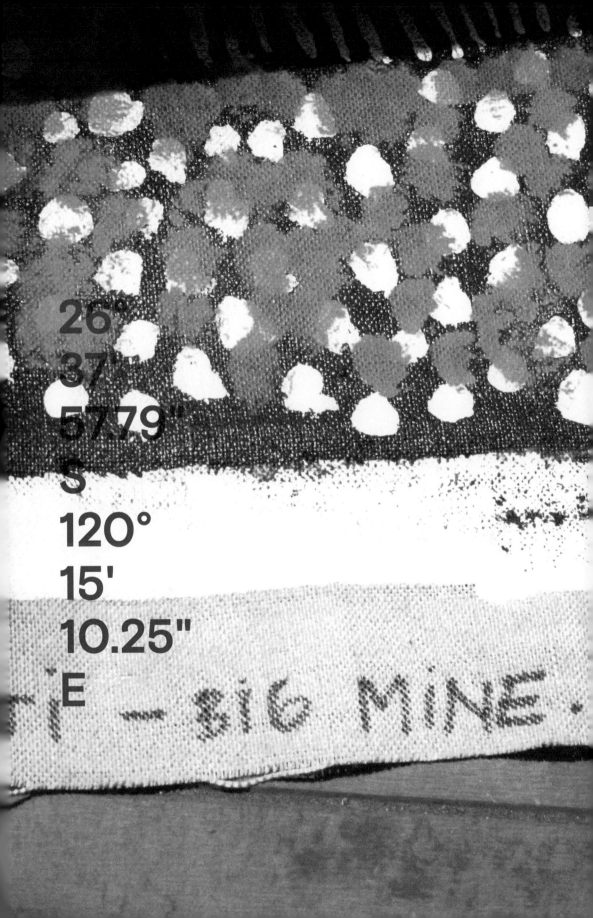

26°
37'
57.79"
S
120°
15'
10.25"
E

Ochre is the Dried Up Blood of Ancient Creatures

Words by Indigenous Australian author
Tyson Mowarin

'In the long darkness the cold wind blows across
the mountain peaks, strong and wild, showing
no mercy for what lies in its path. This new
landscape is born. The very first light shines on
the high peaks; young, wild and free but still
soft… for this is the beginning of time.'

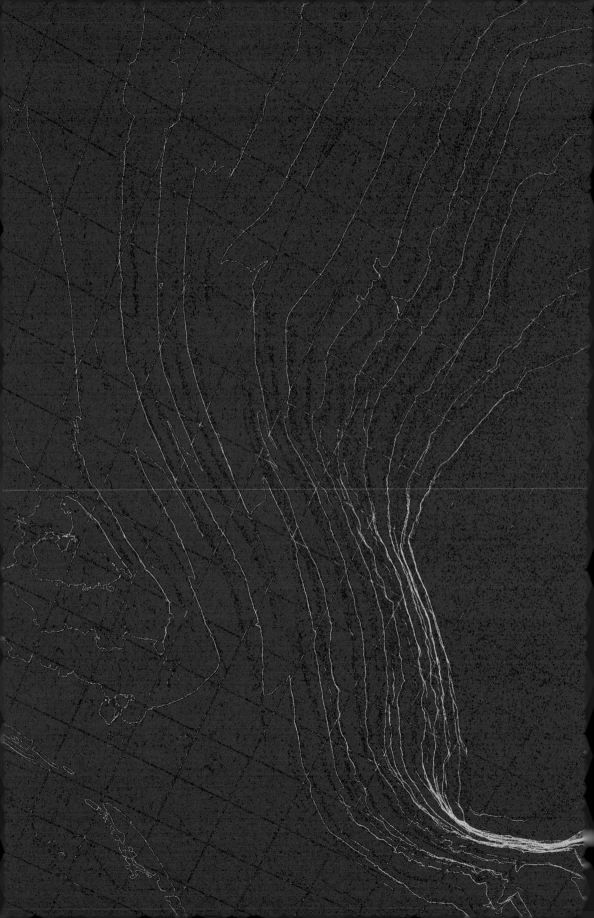

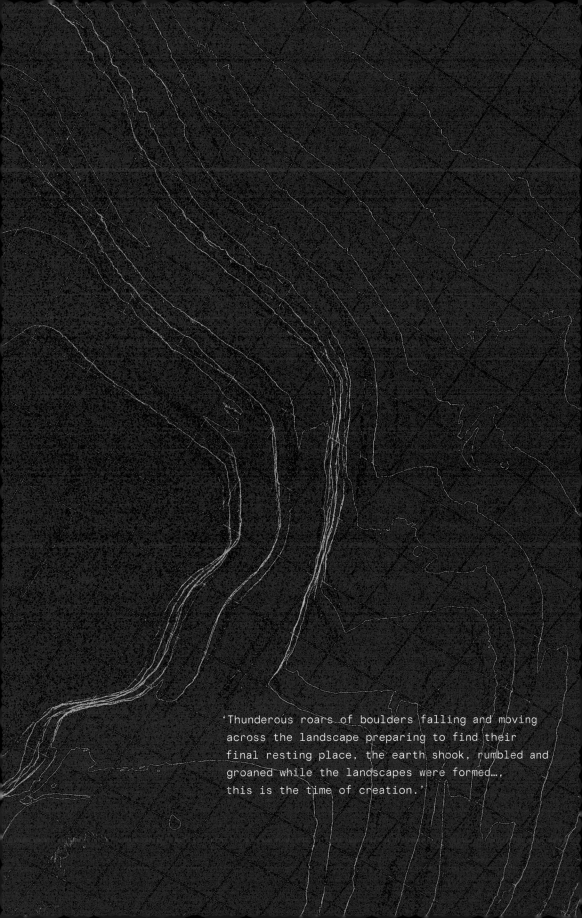

'Thunderous roars of boulders falling and moving
across the landscape preparing to find their
final resting place, the earth shook, rumbled and
groaned while the landscapes were formed…,
this is the time of creation.'

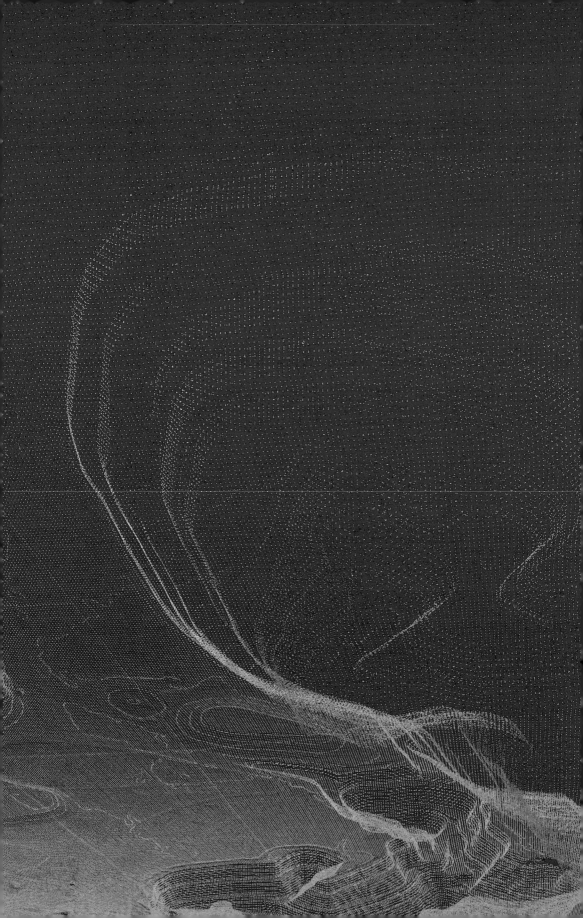

'The land has a living spirit, she hears, she
sees, she feels. The spirit of the land has
always been alive. She hears you when you are
out enjoying her presence and She also hears the
silence when you are not. She sees you and enjoys
your beauty and she feels when you care for her,
she feels pain when you hurt her and is lonely
when she is by herself.'

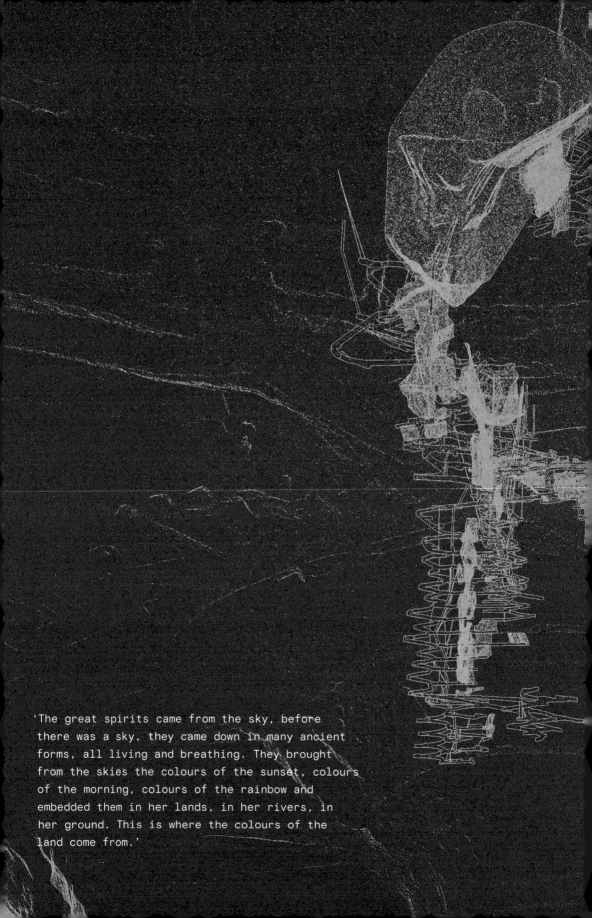

'The great spirits came from the sky, before
there was a sky, they came down in many ancient
forms, all living and breathing. They brought
from the skies the colours of the sunset, colours
of the morning, colours of the rainbow and
embedded them in her lands, in her rivers, in
her ground. This is where the colours of the
land come from.'

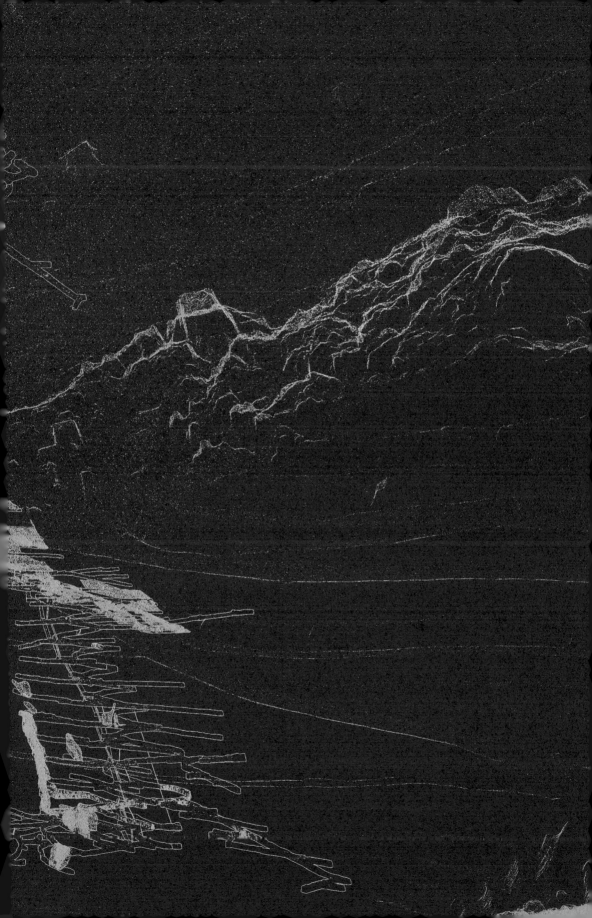

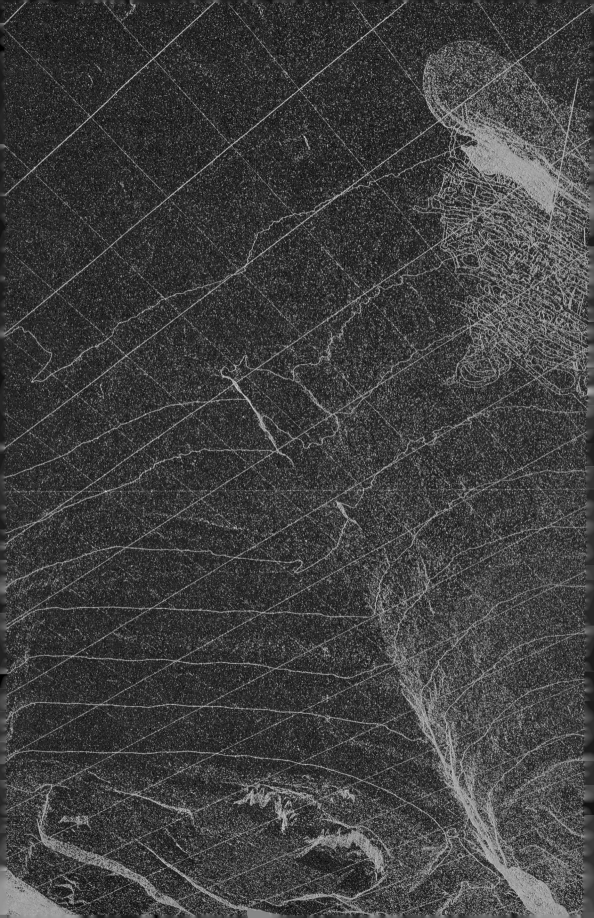

'When the landscapes were young the lands were forming their ancient structures, rolling, tearing, ripping and hiding and revealing themselves. These forces and their journeys coincide with Aboriginal stories of creation.'

'Right across our ancient lands, from the sand
islands and Great Barrier Reef in the east to
the ancient landscapes that form the Murujuga
or Burrup Peninsula in the west of Australia,
where the world's biggest and most comprehensive
petroglyph rock art gallery lives, the stories
of creation times are eerily accurate and reflect
what we see in the land today.

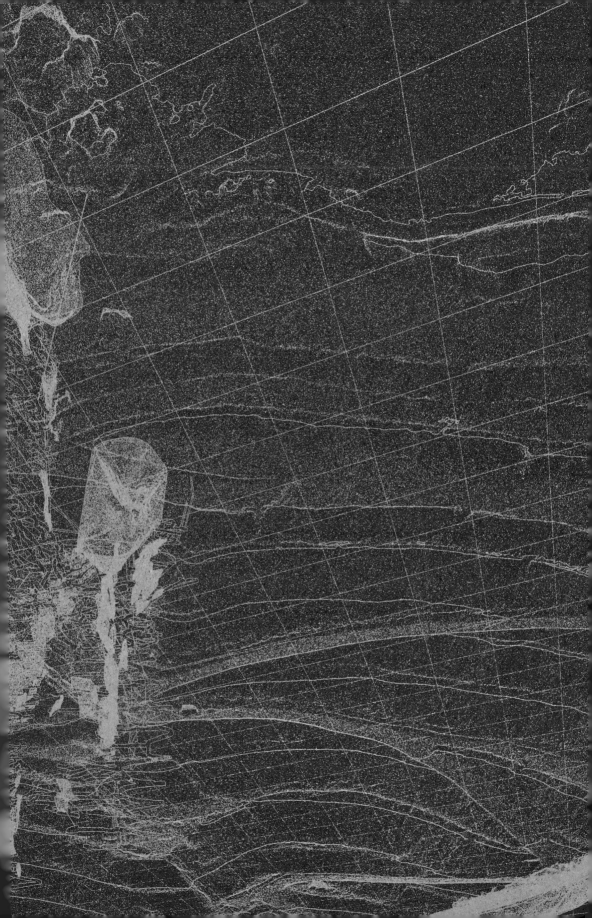

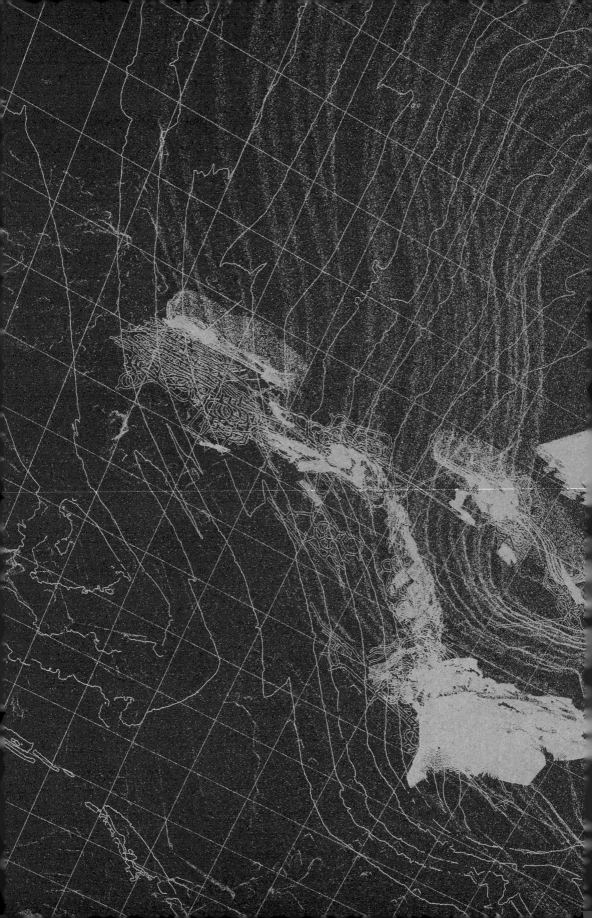

'There are stories of fierce battles, man vs man and spirit vs man and ancient creation gods that fought an almost mythical monster, slaying each other and leaving huge deposits of blood that turned into our blood-red ochre, or the charcoal remains of an ancient animal or forest that turned into coal and eventually diamonds. The tears of a sky god that flooded ancient landscapes, forming the places we see today.'

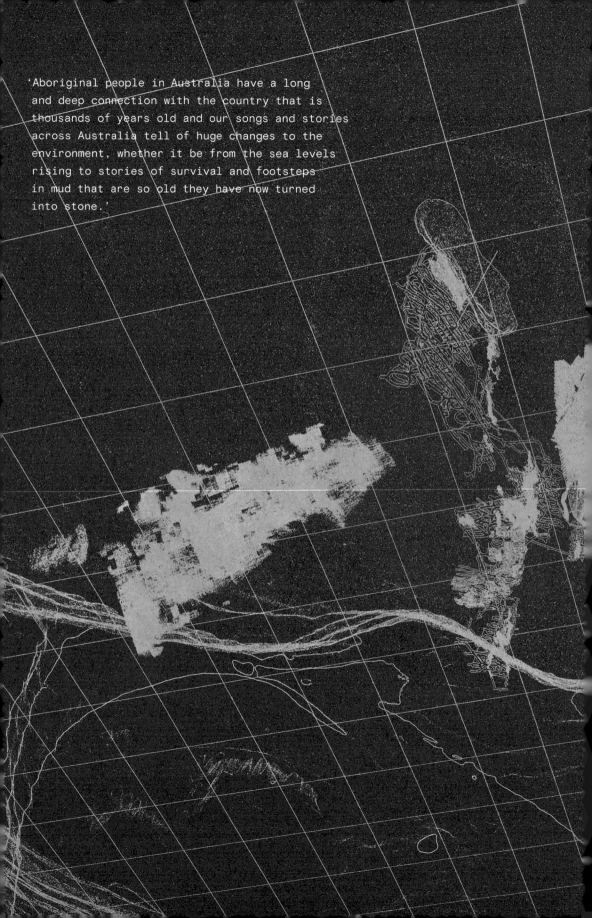

'Aboriginal people in Australia have a long
and deep connection with the country that is
thousands of years old and our songs and stories
across Australia tell of huge changes to the
environment, whether it be from the sea levels
rising to stories of survival and footsteps
in mud that are so old they have now turned
into stone.'

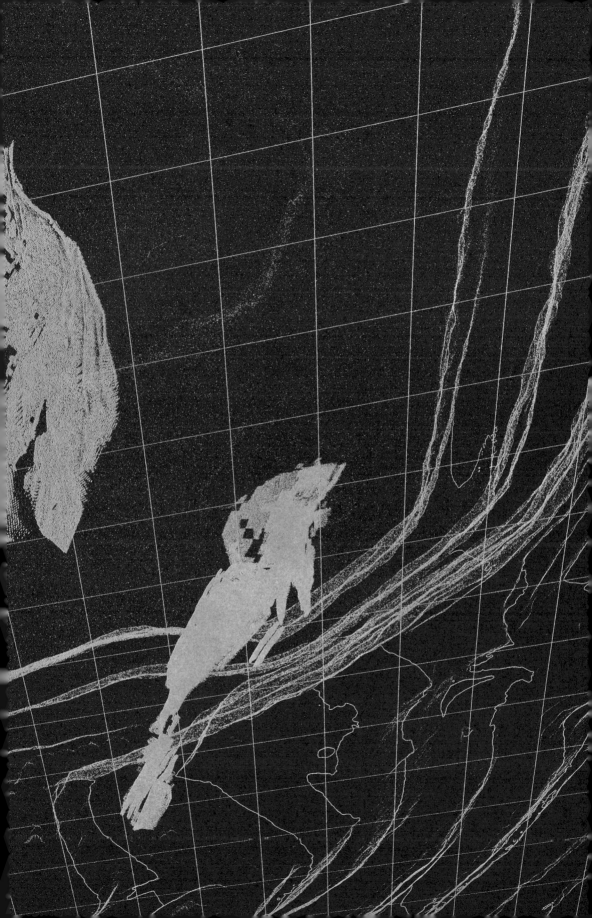

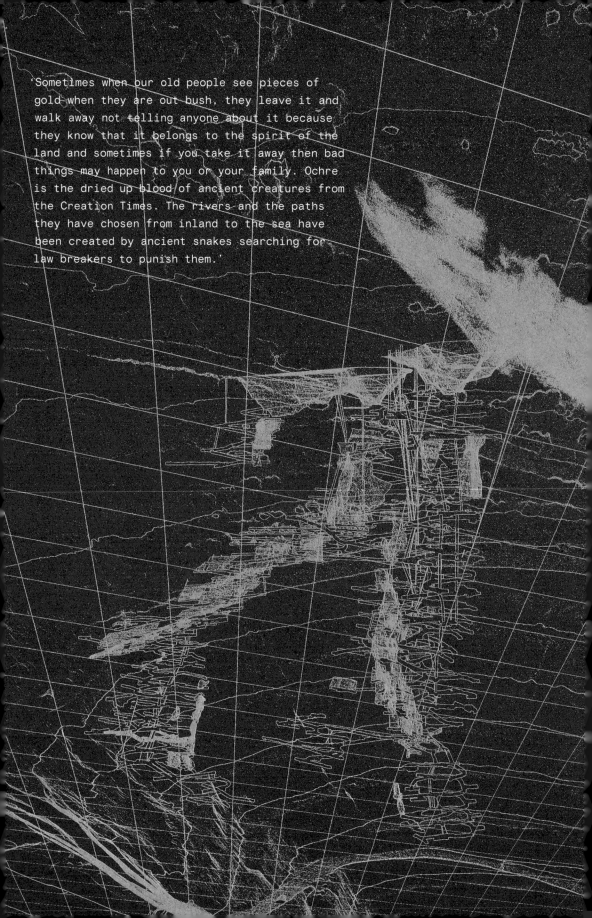

'Sometimes when our old people see pieces of
gold when they are out bush, they leave it and
walk away not telling anyone about it because
they know that it belongs to the spirit of the
land and sometimes if you take it away then bad
things may happen to you or your family. Ochre
is the dried up blood of ancient creatures from
the Creation Times. The rivers and the paths
they have chosen from inland to the sea have
been created by ancient snakes searching for
law breakers to punish them.'

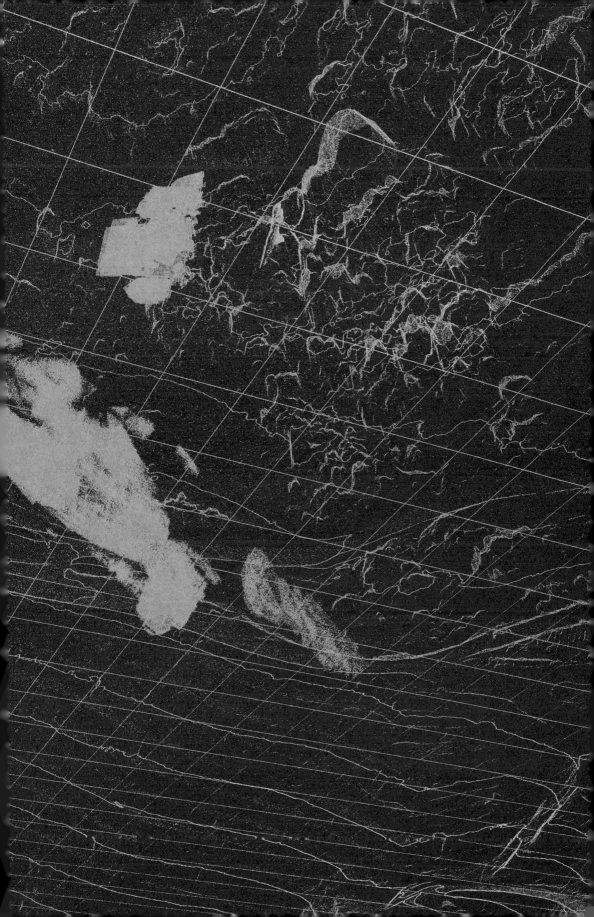

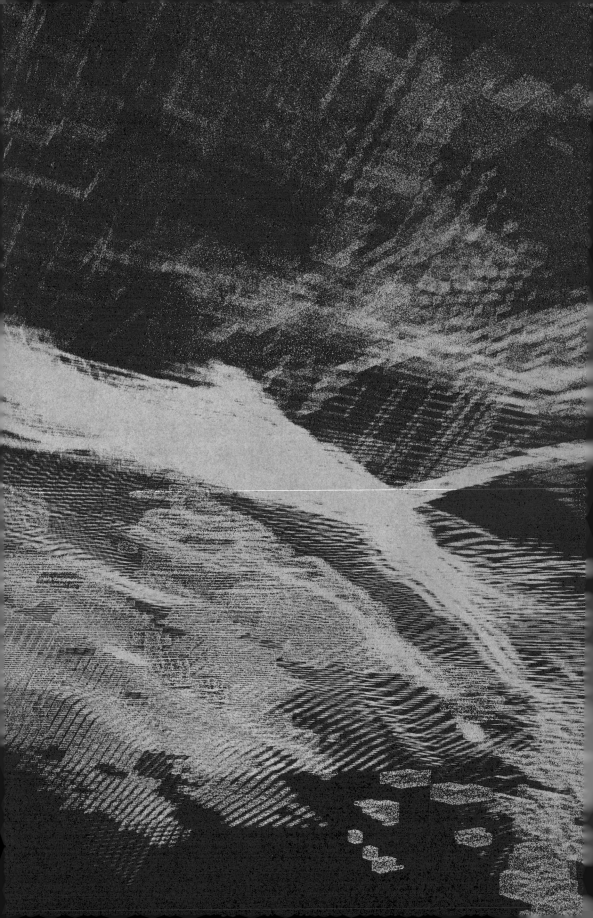

'The way that minerals are deposited across the lands and have been covered up during creation have all got a reason for being where they are. They all have a reason for their existence and a story.'

28°
39'
54.1"
S
119°
10'
56.4"
E

'Having open-cut mines and underground mines hurt the spirit of the land, she sees it, she feels it, she wonders why as she sits and cries, why are we scraping her skin, why are we taking her story?'

By Tyson Mowarin

16 g   8 g   4 g

2g

One of the principle uses of gold is as an
investment instrument. A proxy for accumulated
wealth, a high stakes version of the wad of cash
under the mattress. Much of the gold extracted
from this ancient ground is done so purely so it
can be quantified and weighed. It is then shipped
across the world from one hole in the ground
to another, stored below the surface once more
in the vaults of HSBC or the federal reserve,
Here it remains, to be traded virtually. The
gold price is a culturally constructed value,
a financial fiction, embodied in a block of
material which has been wrung like blood from
a stone – two grams from a tonne of earth on
average. In the cool calculations of the digital
mine model, the shape of the excavation changes
as the variable gold price is entered into the
software. As the gold price rises it becomes
more economical to mine areas of lower gold
ore concentration. The model reveals the various
grades of a single gold ore-body in grams per
tonne and as the price drops the virtual mine
shrinks as the software focuses around deposits
of richer gold ore. One cut at a time, the
fluctuations of the gold price are etched into
the ground of Western Australia, forging deep
underground caverns and open pit excavations
the scale of the Grand Canyon. That steamy black
void in which Unknown Fields stood is a live
graph, shaped by the frequency of electronic
trades in London and New York and from such
distances we can so dramatically affect a
landscape that doesn't belong to us.

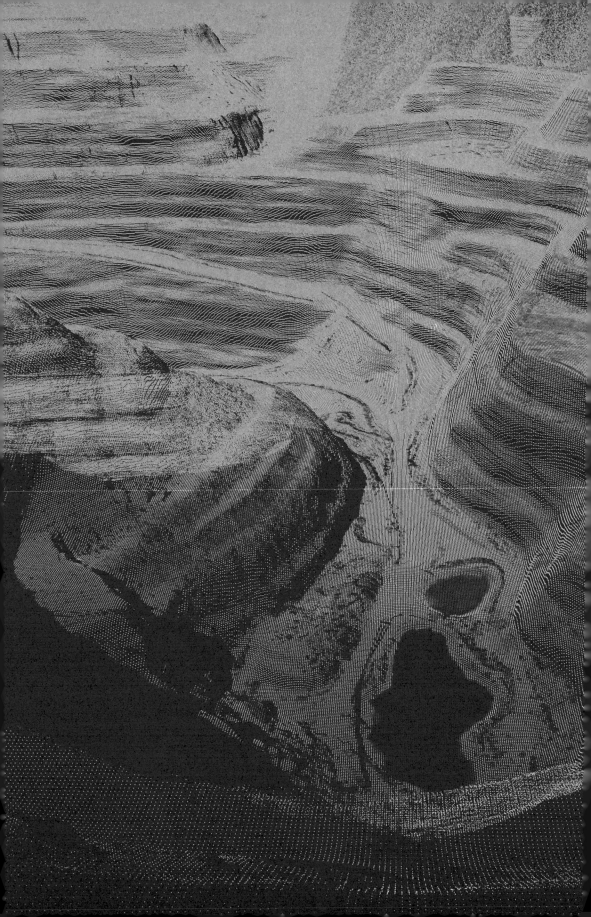

28°
47'
51.1"
S
117°
56'
37.8"
E

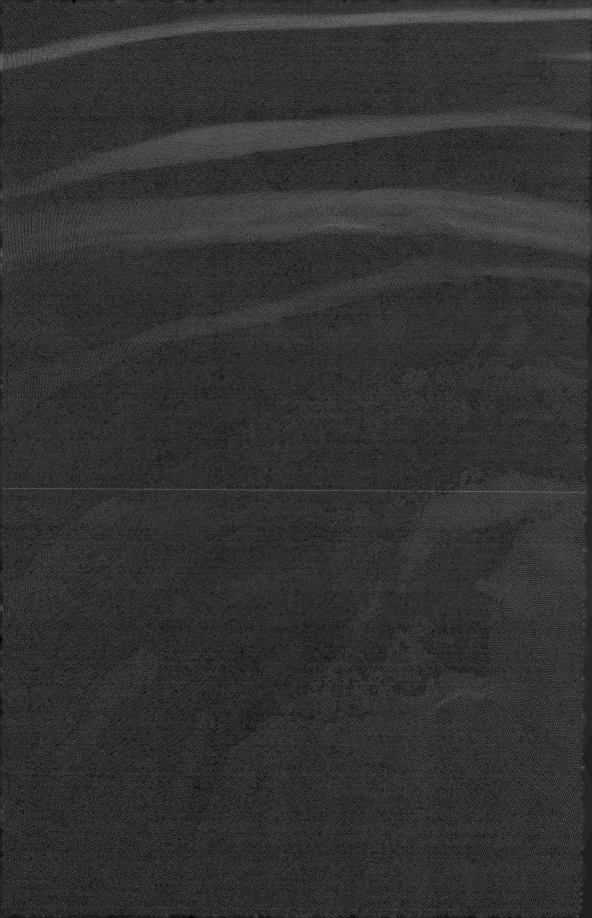

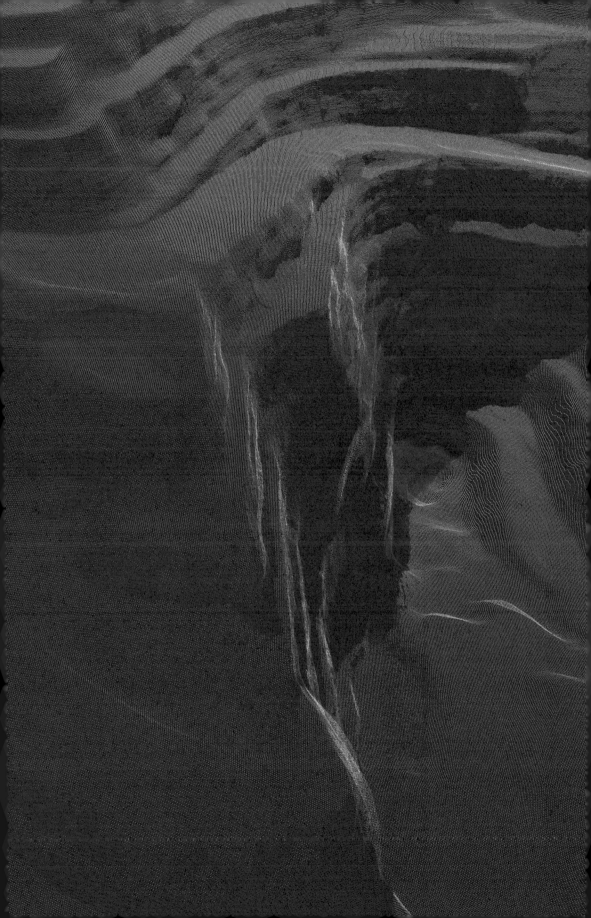

All Mine

Unknown Fields have built a domestic mining machine with a data connection to the precious metals market. A numbers game that carves mountains across the other side of the world is brought home to live with us in more familiar territories. It is live-linked to the gold price as it trades: $1302, $1320, $1314 per ounce. Tracking its percentage rise and fall, the miner carves into the everyday. The abstractions of buying and selling play out in our comfortable mundane, excavating our domestic landscapes.

The financial foundations of the lives we
lead and the things we own are propped up on
investment commodities and the fluctuating values
assigned to them. This abstract stream of numbers
and the distant landscapes they carve are both
obscure alien realms. You sit at your kitchen
table, it mines, the price rises, your world is
excavated as you sip your coffee as you read the
morning papers. It mines as you sleep, as you
take a bath, as you watch TV. What was once out
of sight, lost to distance, just a sacrificial
territory in a place we will never visit is now
bought home, screeching and drilling into the
cities and spaces we all know so well.

    The landscape of Australia is both
everywhere and nowhere. Here in the red ochre of
the Never Never we are carving our desires into
the archaeological record, a new creation story
for our endless city.

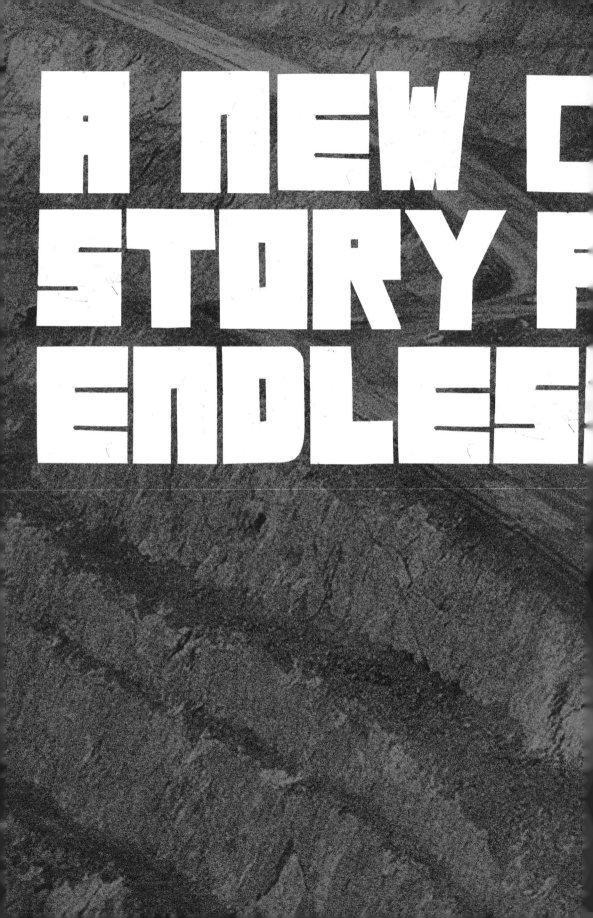

A NEW C
STORY F
ENDLES

Never Never Lands by Unknown Fields

Design: Neasden Control Centre & City Edition Studio
Illustration: Neasden Control Centre

Printed in Italy by Musumeci
ISBN 978-1-907896-85-9

For a catalogue of AA Publications visit
aaschool.ac.uk/publications or email publications@aaschool.ac.uk

AA Publications
36 Bedford Square
London
WC1B 3ES
t + 44 (0)20 7887 4021
f + 44 (0)20 7414 0783

9 781907 896859